Elliott Carter

Figment IV

for Solo Viola

HENDON MUSIC

BOOSEY & HAWKES

AN IMAGEM COMPANY

DISTRIBUTED BY

HAL•LEONARD®
CORPORATION
7777 W. BLUEMOUND RD. P.O. BOX 13819 MILWAUKEE, WI 53213

www.boosey.com
www.halleonard.com

Published by Hendon Music, Inc.
A Boosey & Hawkes company
229 West 28st Street, 11th Fl.
New York NY
10001

www.boosey.com

Notesetting by Thomas Brodhead, B.M.T. Systems, Inc.
First printed June 2007
Second impression with revisions December 2007
Third impression with imprint page February 2010

COMPOSER'S NOTE

Figment IV was written for the wonderful violist, Samuel Rhodes, who performs so brilliantly with the Juilliard Quartet. All of my quartets profited greatly by his unflagging skills and interest.

He gave *Figment IV* its premiere at the Freer Gallery, Washington, D.C. on March 18, 2008.

– Elliott Carter

Duration: 3 minutes

for Sam Rhodes

FIGMENT IV
for Viola

Elliott Carter
(2007)

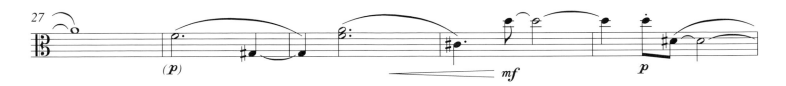

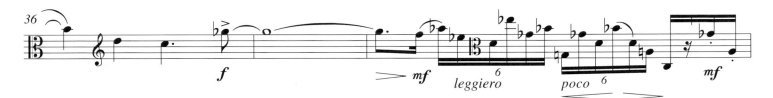

NYC
6 June 2007